A Brief Study of British Defence Policy 1914 – 2005

By Barry Vale

Preface

Is there a requirement for the United Kingdom to maintain and develop a key strategic deterrent beyond Trident and if so, what should it be, could it be non-nuclear and will it be affordable?

The United Kingdom has previously developed and maintained a series of key strategic deterrents. The latest of these strategic deterrents is the Trident submarine based ballistic nuclear missile system that entered service in1994. The United Kingdom as will be examined has not always had a nuclear strategic deterrent, which have only been in existence since 1945. The historical background of the United Kingdom's military and naval past and how that contributed towards the maintenance and development of the British nuclear strategic deterrent and whether those fundamental military requirements will continue shall be discussed and analysed. The reasons for the maintaining and development of the United Kingdom's nuclear and non-nuclear strategic deterrents will form the basis of the arguments outlined below. Although this work will mainly concentrate upon the military criteria for the United Kingdom to maintain and develop a key strategic deterrent that will eventually replace the Trident system not all the considerations are military ones.

Introduction

However where relevant or apt other criteria such as political considerations, changes in the strategic situations and economic factors can impact on whether the United Kingdom finds a nuclear or non-nuclear replacement for the Trident system, if at all. The strategic and military situations as will be mentioned have changed radically since it was decided that Trident, after some delays eventually would replace the aged Polaris missile system. Considering that Trident took 14 years to enter service after it was first ordered and that it takes around five years to build each ballistic nuclear missile submarine the United Kingdom government will probably have to start considering a replacement system within the next five years. That would be so that Trident is not outdated by the time its replacement is completed. The intentions of the United States towards replacing its Trident systems will also be discussed given the close links between the two countries with regard to the development and maintenance of nuclear weapons and their delivery systems.

Originally England and later the United Kingdom maintained and developed the ships of the Royal Navy as its key strategic deterrent. The Royal Navy protected the homeland whilst giving the United Kingdom the vital strategic, economic and naval flexibility to trade with or conquer almost any country in the world. The United Kingdom seemed to always emerge on the winning sides during the numerous wars of the 18th century, due to the strength of the Royal Navy. The loss of the American colonies was hastened by the French gaining control of the sea. The might of the Royal Navy meant that the United Kingdom did not have to have a large standing army with millions of men like France, Germany and Russia. The United Kingdom did not have to become involved in any European wars unless it wanted to, just one in fact between 1815 and 1914 (the Crimean War of 1854-56). The Royal Navy allowed British governments the relative luxury of feeling safe at home and being able to match any power abroad. Britain's isolation from firm diplomatic and military alliances reduced as the cost of maintaining the Royal Navy increased. For example the 1902 naval alliance with

Japan showed the willingness to co-operate to avoid being over stretched. The most important links were those made with France and Russia over fears of German ambitions.

Chapter One 1905 - 1945

However there were limits to what the Royal Navy's power could do as a key strategic deterrent or as an instrument of military and naval policy. If the United kingdom became involved in major European or world conflicts it had to find allies or expand its army, or possibly both. The Royal Navy allowed the British the option to fight on alone if need be; yet it could not guarantee victory by itself. For instance, Trafalgar may have been the Royal Navy's greatest victory yet it still took another decade to finally defeat Napoleon at Waterloo. The British naval blockade was largely ineffective due to the continental system adopted by the French. Prior to the emergence of nuclear weapons no strategic deterrent was entirely effective because they lacked the power to completely destroy any potential enemy.

The potential threat of the Royal Navy did not deter the German military from its plans to invade France in 1914, instead they gambled on a quick victory in the West before the British and Russians could decisively intervene. The Royal Navy did manage to ferry the British Army across to France with surprising speed. The British Army bolstered French defences enough to stop a swift German victory. The gamble of the German generals failed and meant that Germany had to fight on two fronts as well as enduring the Royal Navy blockade which became increasingly effective as the First World War dragged on. The United Kingdom had more strategic options when it controlled the seas yet it also had greater responsibilities. Whether at the start of the 20th century or at the start of the 21st century the United Kingdom has believed that the Royal Navy has the strike power to deter war and spare the burden of military conflict. Replacing the Trident system would be in the same mould as replacing old battleships a century ago, appearing to be strong to avoid major wars.

The United Kingdom started the 20th century at the zenith of its imperial power, maintaining its vast Empire through its trading links and the awesome might of the Royal Navy. That is what put Britain foremost amongst the Great Powers despite the small size of the peacetime British Army. The grave financial, military and naval costs of the First World War removed the United Kingdom from its previous position as the foremost world power although it remained without doubt a Great Power. The British had been on the winning side yet that victory was an expensive one. Aside from the bloody stalemate of the Western Front, the First World War witnessed technological advances that would alter the nature of warfare and offer alternative strategic deterrents. These were the tank and although not entirely new submarines and aircraft. The Germans had carried out bombing raids on London, which had caused widespread outrage if not damage. An almost immediate consequence was the separation of British fighters and bombers from the army and the Royal Navy into the Royal Air Force and the realisation that air power was strategically vital as a deterrent as well as for defensive and offensive means. The United Kingdom's geographical location has not changed yet more advanced weaponry has made it more vulnerable to attack. Upgrading or replacing Trident would be a continuation of previous modernisation programmes aimed at keeping the United Kingdom free of major conflict and providing as much protection from any attacks as possible. In the Inter-war period the Royal Navy remained the key strategic deterrent of the United Kingdom although the emergence of air power as a means to bomb any enemy into submission was considered as a deterrent as well. Despite losing its naval primacy to the United States Navy, the Royal Navy still seemed impressive especially in the shape of the battlecruiser HMS Hood that flew the flag on numerous tours. In reality all three services were starved of cash and new equipment until the re-emergence of the German threat after the Nazis took power in the 1930s. In a similar way the Trident submarines and any replacement ballistic submarines are or will be symbolic of British power, although the Royal Navy is less willing to show them off in public.

Ironically enough given his previous role in building up the Royal Navy's battleship strength during the Anglo-German naval arms race, it was Winston Churchill that was responsible for some of the biggest defence cuts as Chancellor of the Exchequer. The Inter-war period brought economic down turns and reduced trade whilst the skills and factories needed to develop, maintain and produce the weapons that could form key strategic deterrents was curtailed.

However the United Kingdom simply could not afford to be involved in the naval arms race that began to emerge in the immediate aftermath of the war's finish between Japan and the United States. Fears that such a naval build up would be as unsettling and destabilising as the Anglo-German naval arms race led to the Washington Naval Treaty. That treaty placed restrictions on battleship numbers and their size. These restrictions led the Royal Navy, the United States Navy and the Japanese Navy further developing the aircraft carrier, developments in which the British performed a key role. Aircraft carriers gave navies an extra dimension in forming viable fighting forces and strategic deterrents.

The peace treaties at the end of the First World War had given the United Kingdom more territories in the guise of the League of Nations protectorates in Iraq and Palestine. Such gains were better in theory than in practice and further drained the military and naval resources of the United Kingdom. The United Kingdom did not at this point further develop key strategic deterrents and merely spread the military and naval forces it had ever more sparsely across its empire. At least the British had gained from the peace treaties, the Germans in particular lost territory and had strict limits placed on their military and navy forces. They were banned outright from having tanks, submarines and military aircraft. If the Germans had been forced to stay effectively disarmed then perhaps further conflict could have been avoided. However the real winners of the First World War were the United States and Japan that had done comparatively little fighting for their gains. The United Kingdom and France would be left to police world affairs in the Inter-war period due to the isolationism of the United States whilst the future Axis powers of Germany, Italy and Germany were unhappy with their lot after the First World War. As already mentioned Germany had been stripped of all military power by the Versailles settlement yet co-operated with the Soviet Union to test and develop weapons in secret.

Assuming that Germany would remain unarmed allowed the British Treasury to instigate the ten-year rule and curtail the maintenance and development of effective key strategic deterrents. The ten-year rule maintained that the United Kingdom would remain free from major conflicts for a decade. In July 1928 Winston Churchill the rule for another ten years whilst continuing his efforts to cut military spending. The military and political validity of the ten-year rule would be undermined and eventually reversed because of Hitler's foreign and military policies. Sometimes conflicts are easily predictable and sometimes they appear to occur out of the blue, yet armed forces that maintain effective modern equipment with highly skilled personnel are more likely to deter or win victory in such conflicts. An important lesson from military history is that is better to deter conflict from a position of strength than it is from a position of weakness. The British government will probably find the money and resources to replace the Trident system. No government would wish to appear that it would have to appease any other state in a crisis or be held to ransom by any terrorist groups that obtained nuclear weapons.

Whilst it was unlikely that Hitler would have been deterred by the British use of strategic deterrents such deterrents may have stopped the aggression of Italy and Japan. The United Kingdom did nothing to stop the Japanese attacks against China even though there were British colonies in the area. The Royal Navy could have denied the Italians access to the Suez Canal and enforced the League of Nations sanctions after they invaded Abyssinia. The Italians would have been no matches for the Royal Navy. British forces during the Second World War easily outfought them even when the Italians had superior forces. The policy of appeasement had been adopted mainly to delay war long enough to allow the United Kingdom to rearm. Appeasement was also a result of the French being unwilling to act aggression without British support. The United Kingdom's military weaknesses were there for Germany and Japan to take notice of. The Germans knew that the British Army and the RAF were weak whilst the Japanese noticed that the Royal Navy was too stretched to cover or protect all British interests across the globe. For the Japanese the only power that could realistically deter them was the United States as it would take Royal Navy around two months to reinforce the British presence in the Pacific region. The lack of military and naval power available was bad enough yet it was the lack of assertiveness from British and French politicians that undermined peace and nullified the strengths of their respective strategic deterrents the Royal Navy and the French Army. The British government believing that the French Army could look after itself and that the Japanese would refrain from further conquest in the Far East needed to be rearmed first. It was hoped that its fighters could deal with any German bombers whilst the threat of British bombing raids would deter the Germans. The British government's hopes that rearmament would deter the Germans and prevent another war were unfulfilled. However rearmament was a slow and expensive process.. However the best way of averting the Second World War would have avoided the need for costly rearmament, that would have been the British and French stopping Hitler's remilitarization of the Rhineland in 1936. The lessons learnt from the 1930s are that strategic deterrents need updating on a regular basis and that other countries have to believe they are effective and that the British government will not give in to unacceptable demands. Deterrence is only possible from positions of strength and when it is backed up by military and political determination not to give in.

The Second World War would prove even more costly and destructive than the First World War. Not only was the scale of the military conflict much greater, the military, political and strategic consequences were far more profound. The death toll was far higher due to the ideological undertones of the conflict, the deliberate targeting of civilians and the technological advance of weaponry. For the United Kingdom most of the period between 1939 and 1942 was a series of one defeat after another. British forces were not able to prevent the rapid defeat of Poland, Norway, the Low Countries and most spectacularly of all France. The failure to defend Norway could have cost Winston Churchill his job at the Admiralty yet instead it cost Neville Chamberlain his job, replaced by the more dynamic Churchill. The one positive to come out of the Norwegian campaign was the heavy losses of the German Navy. The fall of France was remarkably swift being due as much too superior tactics and strategy of the Germans as much as the quality of their weapons. Had the Germans managed to stop the evacuation from Dunkirk and gained control of the French Navy the United Kingdom's fate could have been sealed. The British were left to fight on alone knowing that the Germans had gained the strategic advantages of being able to launch air and naval attacks from French and Norwegian bases. British survival in the Battle of Britain lifted the immediate threat of invasion although the RAF could not stop the heavy bombing of London and other cities. The RAF had survived due to the use of radar, the quality of its fighters and the bravery of its pilots. In the Middle East and Mediterranean the British had taken Tripoli on land and badly damaged the Italian fleet with the daring air raid against Taranto. Yet the prospects of victory looked bleak until the entries of the Soviet Union and the United States into the war during 1941. However the Royal Navy found it a great strain to send supplies to the Soviet Union via its Arctic convoys as well as facing U-boat attacks in the Atlantic. Japan's entry into the war brought further heavy losses, that of Hong Kong, Singapore and Burma coupled with the sinking of the Prince of Wales and Repulse. The fall of Singapore was Britain's worst single defeat ever whilst the loss of the Prince of Wales and Repulse clearly showed the need for air cover in any military and naval operation. The British would make a great contribution towards the total victory of the Allies particularly Western Europe, the Middle East and in the Far East. They would have made a greater contribution to the victory against Japan had the American use of atomic bombs not shortened the war.

Through a great deal of effort and the sacrifice of millions of lives (especially Soviet ones) the Allies overcame their disastrous starts to the Second World War. In the end their superior numbers, greater firepower and industrial capacities paved the way for eventual victory. The RAF's Bomber Command had argued that a strategic bombing campaign against Germany would shorten the war. The bombing campaign disrupted German arms production and devastated cities like Berlin and Dresden. In defeat the Germans had developed or further refined weapons that would play an important part in the development of nuclear strategic deterrents. These were the ballistic missile in the shape of the V2 rockets used against London plus the improvements to diesel electric submarines with a much greater range than previously seen. If such submarines had been available at the start of the war then perhaps the Germans would have succeeded in severing British supply routes. Once submarines became nuclear powered they offered the stealthiest means of launching nuclear missiles. In a strategic and territorial sense the world altered considerably as a result of the Second World War, alterations that affected the United Kingdom's position and status thus influencing changes in the military's and government's concepts with regard to key strategic deterrents. The United States and the Soviet Union were now the world's strongest countries. They were so much stronger than all the other powers, that the term superpower was first used in the immediate post-war period.

As a consequence of its titanic struggle against Nazi Germany the Soviet Union had gained control over much of Central and Eastern Europe whilst the Big Four (the United States, the Soviet Union, Britain plus France) split control of Germany and Austria between them. The actual damage sustained by Britain and much of Western Europe was greater than during the First World War. The scale of devastation in the Soviet Union and Eastern Europe was even greater. The cost of post-war reconstruction would far be very high and perhaps a sharp curtailment of military expenditure would be the best means to fund that reconstruction. The new government of Clement Atlee was therefore faced with many problems such as starting the process of de-colonisation and it intended to reduce defence spending to pay for its social reform programmes. Demobilisation could not have been as widespread as it had been after 1918, as the United Kingdom had to retain its forces in its zone of occupied Germany. Such was the devastation in the British zone that the British Army had to feed the German population to avert starvation. The United Kingdom's financial position was already precarious and was worsened once the Americans end the Lend – Lease scheme that had give the British much of the material and resources to finish the war. However aside from the men that remained in Germany the British Army was still involved in fighting or attempting peacekeeping in Greece, India, Malaya and Palestine. The growing tension between the Soviet Union and the United States developed into the Cold War which meant that the United Kingdom had to consider the development and maintenance of a key strategic deterrent rather than disarming to the levels of the Inter-war period. Conversely the end of the Cold War has given the British government the option to scale down or discard the nuclear deterrent after Trident is withdrawn from service.

So far the biggest change caused by the Second World War that had the greatest impact on the United Kingdom's post-war maintenance and development of a key strategic deterrent has only been alluded to, that was the emergence of the atomic bomb. Winston Churchill had known about the United States' development of the atomic bomb. Churchill fearing that the Germans might develop one first had allowed British scientists to work on the Manhattan Project. During the early phase of the war British scientists' research level was on a par with the Americans. The idea to carry out the project in the United States was due to the greater test facilities available and from the point of view that it was out of the range of German bombs.

Whilst President Franklin Roosevelt had a strong relationship with Churchill, that closeness did not develop between Churchill and Truman or indeed when Atlee replaced Churchill. Perhaps Truman understood the military and strategic consequences of using atomic bombs. He was therefore unwilling to share nuclear technology with any other nation, even the British that had made a telling contribution to its initial development were excluded. Aside from developing the atomic bomb on their own British scientists failed to match their American and Soviet counterparts. That failure has meant there is a tendency to rely on the Americans for the maintenance and development of nuclear deterrents that has persisted for more than 50 years and will continue should Trident be replaced.

The use of the atomic bombs against Japan in August 1945 had certainly hastened the end of the Second World War as it had been intended to do. Truman had wished to save the lives of American forces and the earlier end of the war also had the advantage of preventing Soviet forces entering the Asia Pacific region to attack Japan. The United States ended the war as the world's sole nuclear power, which gave it an immediate military and strategic advantage over every country in the world, especially the Soviet Union, the United Kingdom and France. The Soviet Union felt insecure that it did not have its own atomic bombs. Stalin was determined that the Soviet Union would be the next nuclear power thus contributing to worsening relations with the West and the onset of the Cold War. To start with only the Americans had the resources and the knowledge to build atomic bombs, resources that the Soviets, British and French would find more difficult to require, although they managed to find the knowledge to make atomic weapons with less difficulty. The Americans became even less willing to co-operate with the British to let them maintain and develop nuclear weapons as a key strategic deterrent. That reluctance was especially strong when the Americans believed British scientists and security services were giving the Soviet Union nuclear secrets that accelerated the Soviet production of nuclear weapons.

Chapter Two The Decision to go Nuclear

There were certainly good strategic and military reasons for the Atlee government to launch the United Kingdom's nuclear weapons programme as far as it was considered, even if there are mainly financial based reasons for not doing so. Firstly the Atlee government wished to maintain the United Kingdom's position as a Great Power without having to keep the British Empire in tact. Having the atomic bomb it was argued would be the most obvious symbol of that Great Power status continuing when other more established symbols of that status such as the Indian Raj were quickly vanishing into the past. In a way the maintenance and development of nuclear weapons was a pragmatic means to maintain British air, military and naval firepower without having to have wartime levels of conventional weapons and recruitment of military personnel. Although the government managed to demobilise most of the wartime service personnel relatively quickly it was unable to finish national service, as British commitments did not as quickly as intended. When the RAF could drop nuclear weapons more powerful than all the bombs dropped on a 1000 bomber raid there was no longer the need to have a 1000 bombers to wipe out targets when a single bomber could achieve the same results.

However, the United Kingdom did not have the basic infrastructure to produce nuclear weapons and it was expensive to build reprocessing plants as well as obtaining uranium and plutonium. All that took a considerable amount of effort for a nation stretched to breaking point by the cost of the Second World War. It also happened under a Labour government that was committed to extensive domestic social reform and de-colonisation abroad. The United Kingdom would succeed in building its own nuclear weapons yet it was a definite strain on a weak economy. There were certainly those in the British military and government that believed the United Kingdom should have its own nuclear weapons as a key strategic deterrent to deter the Soviet Union yet also to have some independence of action from the Americans. The United Kingdom reached its military and economic limits in 1947 when it could no longer support the Greek government during the Greek civil war. The United States responded by introducing the Marshall Plan to aid

Western economic recovery and through the formation of the North Atlantic Treaty Organisation, Nato. Added to the cost of developing nuclear weapons was the cost of developing and deploying bombers capable of reaching their targets, ensuring that the RAF had fighters capable of stopping Soviet bombers and protection for RAF airbases. The United Kingdom could increase the range of its nuclear weapons by giving the Royal Navy aircraft capable of dropping such weapons for its aircraft carriers. Launching nuclear strikes from aircraft carriers had the advantage that the fleet could keep moving and would be harder to target than airbases. Thus the RAF and Royal Navy needed to obtain the best bombers to be able to drop the bomb. However, as aircraft, ships and submarines become more advanced they become more expensive.

The United Kingdom justified its maintenance and development of nuclear weapons as the key strategic deterrent as being made necessary due to the Cold War and to help the Americans maintain parity or a lead over the Soviet Union in the total numbers of nuclear weapons each side had. The high cost of having nuclear weapons was to be compared to the higher cost of allowing the Soviet Union to gain control of Western Europe or to blackmail the United Kingdom into doing what Moscow wanted. In other words having nuclear weapons that the United Kingdom would remain a powerful nation that would not have to appease any other nation due to its own weaknesses. To some extent the United Kingdom reduced its commitments in its attempts to reduce its weaknesses. The withdrawals from India, Palestine and Greece were sensible as they stopped the United Kingdom from going bankrupt.

The Cold War developed in such a way as to make governments on either side of the divide doubt the other's intentions and to suspect the worst. Communism seemed to be an increasingly dangerous threat to the United States and Western Europe. The communist threat and the Cold War provided the rationale for British governments to consider the maintenance and development of nuclear weapons as the country's key strategic deterrent. The Berlin blockade, the Greek civil war, and the emergence of communist guerrilla forces in Malaya and Indo-China. The communist take-overs in China and North Korea led to fears of a domino effect in

Asia. The North Koreans would heat up the Cold War considerably by invading South Korea. The United Kingdom joined the United Nation forces that rallied to the aid of South Korea. The Korean War escalated when China joined in on the North Korean side. Involvement in the Korean War pushed up British defence expenditure yet it provided incentives to ensure that the forces kept their weapons up to date and as powerful as possible. The Korean War also made the United States happier to aid the United Kingdom in its maintenance and development of a nuclear based key strategic deterrent as part of the West's containment of communism policy which the Americans termed the 'Truman Doctrine'. The Atlee government established the main pillars of post-war foreign and defence policies; the strengthening of the Atlantic alliance and a nuclear based key strategic deterrent. It also started the trend of always being able to find enough money to maintain and develop nuclear weapons no matter whatever other spending plans had to be dropped or delayed.

Although the Atlee government had contemplated the maintenance and development of a nuclear based key strategic deterrent when it came into office, the final decision for the United Kingdom to go nuclear was not made until 1947. This momentous decision concerning the United Kingdom's foreign and defence policies, was made behind closed doors by the Cabinet. The decision was made behind closed doors to avoid opposition from the traditionally pacifist and anti-nuclear left-wing members of the Labour Party. It was also hoped that secrecy would not alert other countries of British intentions. In his famous Fulton, Missouri speech of 1946 that used the term 'Iron Curtain' for the time, Winston Churchill had also urged the Americans (and by inference the British) to impress the Soviet Union with a strong nuclear force as its main strategic deterrent. By this point Churchill was the Leader of the Opposition and had a greater degree of freedom to express views that he could not have done as Prime Minister. It also shows that the United Kingdom would still have maintained and developed nuclear weapons as the key strategic deterrent if the Conservatives had won the 1945 general election. The only difference may have been the length of time it would have taken to decide to build the atomic bomb.

To make the British atomic bomb reality rather than just a pipe dream the Atlee government turned to the eminent British scientist William Penney. Penney as a veteran of the Manhattan Project had the experience and the knowledge to develop nuclear weapons as the United Kingdom's key strategic deterrent. Penney and his research team would eventually be based at Aldermaston, which would become a focus point for anti-nuclear protesters from the 1950s onwards. Whilst Penney and his team of researchers had the knowledge and developed the expertise to produce atomic bombs relatively quickly it was the lack of weapons grade plutonium and other essential materials that delayed progress towards the United Kingdom becoming the world's third nuclear power. Indeed the United Kingdom's first nuclear power station and processing plant at Windscale had only started to produce weapons grade plutonium during 1951, barely in time for the first British nuclear test at the end of 1952. The United States refused to let the British test their bomb at one of the American test sites and therefore the test was done on an Australian island. The United Kingdom's nuclear weapons were to be potentially used and deployed by its new jet bomber, the Canberra and eventually the Royal Navy's aircraft carrier bombers such as the Sea Vixen. However what some became apparent was that once it had been decided that the United Kingdom needed a nuclear based key strategic deterrent that it had to be constantly maintained and developed or upgraded to avoid becoming obsolete. Upgrades and replacements would make it more expensive to have such a strategic deterrent. In terms of the Cold War the British deterrent was more effective due to the close relationship with the Americans and that any use of those weapons would be closely co-ordinated with the White House and the Pentagon. The Americans will help the British to replace Trident should they continue to think it is in their best military and strategic interest to do so.

The mainstay of the British nuclear deterrent was the RAF's V-bombers. However the Americans and the Soviets had already developed the more powerful H-bombs. The Victors, Valiants and Vulcans were delayed until 1955.
 Even at this early stage of the British nuclear deterrent showed a tendency to become quickly out dated, the V -bombers for instance

were soon countered by improved Soviet surface to air missile defences and jet fighters. The search for aircraft to replace the V-bombers would prove costly and would eventually lead to the decision to adopt Trident's predecessor, the Polaris system. The costs of funding such replacements proved unjustified by the aircraft that were developed. For the British the only way they found to prevent their nuclear deterrent becoming obsolete was to rely on the Americans to supply their technology in the form of Polaris and the later Trident missile systems. The Americans will have to eventually replace Trident as they have had it in service longer. So the United Kingdom will if its past track record is anything to go by decide to replace Trident with the same system with the intention of maintaining nuclear power status.

Polaris and Trident were developed along with rival Soviet systems to survive pre-emptive nuclear strikes from the other side in the event of war. Should the Americans and the British following in their wake decide to replace Trident it would be in favour of a similar submarine based system. As early as the 1950s the British Chiefs of Staff doubted the long-term viability of the British nuclear deterrent being reliant on the planes of the RAF and the Royal Navy surviving Soviet pre-emptive strikes. Land based ballistic missiles were also regarded as being too difficult to protect. Whilst RAF airfields in Britain and West Germany were known to the Soviets they also usually had a good knowledge of where the Royal Navy's aircraft carriers were. The United Kingdom lacked the financial resources to build up the Royal Navy to such an extent to protect its aircraft carriers or to build silos for land based ballistic missiles like the Americans and the Soviets. With hindsight it was sensible that successive British governments did not keep pace with the superpowers in the nuclear arms race. The Soviets usually lagged behind in technological quality yet usually attained parity in terms of quantity. The United Kingdom could in some respects match the technological expertise of the Americans without the ability to develop things fully and no means of increasing its relative strength. The nuclear arms race meant that weapons soon became obsolete, a trend that could possibly have slowed down with Trident as the Cold War finished shortly before the demise of the Soviet Union. The United Kingdom in many respects only stayed and remains a nuclear power as it suits the Americans for this to be the case. The Soviet Union undermined its own existence by competing in the nuclear arms race without having the economic base to sustain it. Even with the Americans co-operating to provide the United Kingdom with all its nuclear deterrents since Polaris and presumably with Trident's successor it has been a strain on British military, naval and economic resources to maintain a nuclear deterrent. The Soviet Navy did develop some of the most powerful hunter-killer submarines that threatened not only the United States Navy battle groups but also American and British ballistic nuclear submarines.

Nato's conventional forces in Western Europe would have been in trouble if the Soviet Union had launched conventional attacks against which is why the United Kingdom and other Nato hoped that the nuclear weapons the Americans, British and French had would be an effective strategic deterrent. Added to the superior quantity land forces was the increasing strength of Soviet Navy especially after its humiliation during the Cuban Missile Crisis of 1962. The Soviet Navy would have posed a considerable threat to British trade and the Royal Navy itself. The United Kingdom's governments however continued to shrink the size of the Royal Navy as its new ships became more expensive and savings had to be made to pay for Polaris and then Trident. Between 1965 and 1968 the Labour government cut all military and naval projects it considered to be impractical or too expensive to ensure that they did not have to cancel the Polaris programme. The most high profile project to be axed was the TSR2 aircraft that had been intended to carry the next generation of free fall British weapons. The new bombs had the advantage of being lighter so and therefore deployed by more aircraft. The government was going to purchase up to 50 American FIII bombers yet that plan was axed to ensure that Polaris could be paid for. In 1981 the defence review introduced deep cuts to the Royal Navy with the exception of the Trident programme, with the unforeseen consequence that Argentina invaded the Falklands War. That conflict showed the value of the Royal Navy's aircraft carriers and nuclear attack submarines and meant the cuts were reversed. The pertinent point here is that once the British government decides that it wants a nuclear replacement for Trident then the funds will be found to pay for it, even if that means cutting back on conventional forces. When faced with a severe recession in the early 1990s the Major government did not save billions of pounds by abandoning Trident when the end of the Cold War meant that the danger of nuclear conflict seemed to have receded. Faced with a similar position when paying for Trident's replacement it is likely that any British government would somehow find means to carry on the United Kingdom's nuclear status.

Many of the improvements and upgrades in the United Kingdom's nuclear based key strategic deterrents can be traced back to the 1958 agreement with the United States to share information and technology. For the United States it seemed a good idea that the United Kingdom should share some of its defence burden during the Cold War. The perceived advantage for the United Kingdom was that the sharing of information and technology allowed the British to remain in the nuclear club. Although the British had some success in developing their own nuclear and conventional weapons, the Ministry of Defence got into the habit of abandoning the development of British weapons to buy the American weapons that already existed. After the V bombers the Lightning and the Harrier were the only planes wholly designed and built by the British to enter service. The Blue Streak missile was withdrawn and TSR2 was abandoned in favour of FIII and Polaris respectively with the FIII orders eventually being cancelled to allow more money to be spent on Polaris. President Kennedy had allowed the British to adopt Polaris after the Nassau agreement of 1962. The Royal Navy had originally wanted five Polaris submarines to enter active service in order for at least one submarine to be fully deployed all the time. Aware of the rising costs linked to the Polaris programme the Treasury reduced the number to four. Although Polaris represented a substantial increase in the power of the United Kingdom key strategic deterrent it had to be upgraded to counter increases in the numbers of Soviet Navy warheads. The United States Navy as an intermediate measure between Polaris and its new Trident system had introduced Poseidon. In the United Kingdom the Callaghan government had faced severe financial difficulties and even had to take out and IMF loan. However, in a secret cabinet meeting the Treasury was available to find the extra £1 billion needed to upgrade Polaris to Chevaline. That decision only came to light because the Thatcher government had aimed to discredit its immediate predecessor and the Treasury would prove to hide such a level of secret military expenditure.

The incoming Thatcher government in May 1979 almost immediately decided the Trident should become the United Kingdom's next nuclear key strategic deterrent and was determined to pay for it no matter how much it cost. This decision took place amidst a background of increasing tension between the superpowers especially after the Soviet invasion of Afghanistan and the election of Ronald Reagan as American president. Aside from the fact that the nuclear strategic deterrent needed periodically upgrading, the Polaris submarines could not remain in service indefinitely as they could need refits more frequently to remain safe. The longer the refits take the longer the United Kingdom's key strategic deterrent is weakened by having fewer submarines on station. Eventually the Trident submarines will face the same problems of increasing maintenance needs and declining time in active Royal Navy service. At some point all four submarines will have to be withdrawn from service as they will not be safe for their crews and be unreliable for the Royal Navy. Extensive refits can keep the Trident submarines in operation for longer yet in the long run the cost of a replacement will have to be met or the United Kingdom nuclear strategic deterrent will have downgraded or abandoned. The British Trident submarines are smaller than their American counterparts and only have two-thirds of the missile launchers, a reflection of the belief that the Royal Navy did not need as many warheads as the United States Navy. Such a reduction in capacity also reduced costs and construction times. Perhaps such amendments to Trident's replacement could be expected. The Royal Navy could not save money by cutting corners on health and safety procedures as those would be dangerous not only to its crews but also for the environment. Poor maintenance of submarines can prove to be more expensive in the long run as crews and submarines can be lost. The Soviet Navy was less concerned about properly maintaining its submarines than the Royal Navy and the United States Navy. The Soviet Navy often ignored safety issues to ensure that the maximum number of hunter killer and ballistic missile submarines was on station during the Cold War. Western navies knew of some submarines being damaged and even sunk as a result of poor maintenance and accidents. It was only after the Cold War that the full cost of ignoring health and safety issues and infrequent refits was 39 damaged and 5 sunk submarines, with a minimum of 300 fatalities.

The Russian Navy has sharply reduced the number of ships and submarines in service compared to the Soviet Navy in its heyday. Such cuts were a direct result of the Russian's lack of money and the START (Strategic Arms Reduction Talks) agreement, which meant that it could decommission the oldest ballistic missile submarines from service. However, the environmentally unsafe and military insecure in which Russia and other former Soviet Union states have dealt with nuclear weapons and waste products had increased over terrorism. Fears for instance that terrorists could gain control of enough nuclear material to build either a nuclear or a so-called dirty bomb that spreads radioactive materials following a conventional explosion. The fear of terrorists having nuclear weapons available to them is a strong argument for the United Kingdom retaining a nuclear based key strategic deterrent system when it eventually needs to replace Trident. The fact that Russia and China still have nuclear weapons needs to be considered with regard to whether Trident's replacement should be a nuclear or non-nuclear based key strategic deterrent system. Russia spends less on less on defence than the Soviet Union did. The Russians spent marginally less on its military than the United Kingdom, some $1.5 billion less in 1999, making them fifth and sixth globally in terms of total military expenditure. Although conflict with Russia might at present seem inconceivable yet it could be a possibility should Russia return to be controlled by an authoritarian regime rather than a democratic one. The Russians however are used to the concept of Mutually Assured Destruction, which means that they would be very unlikely to start a nuclear conflict. The United Kingdom would not probably take the lead as to whether going nuclear was the appropriate step to take. The United Kingdom's independent nuclear deterrent is not as independent as the United Kingdom government would like people believe it is. However given the consequences of using nuclear weapons at a global level such consultation would be sensible, in order to stop unnecessary escalation.

Replacing the Trident system will cost an estimated £15 billion and that will be approved during the lifetime of the present Parliament. Whilst the four Vanguard class Trident submarines should remain in service for at least another two decades it will take approximately 15 years to bring its replacement into service especially if such a replacement was the next generation of ballistic missile submarines. Presently the Treasury allows for the cost of maintaining and updating Trident in each annual defence budget as well as extra money to finance the development and maintenance of Trident's replacement as the key strategic deterrent. The Labour Party manifesto for the 2005 general election confirmed the party leadership's long term commitment to replacing Trident so that the United Kingdom could its key strategic deterrent effective and thus maintaining the nuclear capability well into the 21st century. Just like Polaris and Trident before it Trident's replacement submarines and nuclear warheads being developed and constructed within the United Kingdom to protect jobs at Aldermaston and British ship builders with the missiles probably being American designed. A system based around submarine launched ballistic missiles will almost certainly remain the favoured form of nuclear deterrent both for the United States and therefore the United Kingdom. Although there are probably cheaper nuclear deterrent options such as ground based ballistic missiles or air-launched cruise missiles are considered strategically and military less effective than a submarine based system due to increased vulnerability and shorter ranges respectively.

The post Cold War is not a safer place for all countries compared to the Cold War era. Increased global instability can be used as a reason for all the nuclear powers and not just the United Kingdom to replace and maintain their nuclear deterrents as and when that is needed. The nuclear powers fear that if they down grade or scrap their deterrents they could be black mailed by other states or terrorists that obtain nuclear capability. The United Kingdom will therefore keep its nuclear capabilities to have the flexibility to deal with any such threat. However the nature of conflicts has appeared to change since the end of the Cold War. There have been more civil wars and conflicts that emerged after the break up of the Soviet

Union and Yugoslavia, or in the case of the American led war on terror against organisations rather than nation states. Although the weak armies of Afghanistan were crushed with rapid efficiency insurrectionists inspired and linked with Al-Qaeda are proving more difficult to defeat. Nuclear deterrents may deter states if in enough quantity yet the same weapons are not likely to deter the likes of Al-Qaeda in any event. Nuclear deterrents made no difference to the Al-Qaeda attacks of 9/11 against the United States and the subsequent bombings in London. Al-Qaeda does not have the same rationale as other terrorist organisations and would no doubt use nuclear devices if they ever obtained any. The problem with using nuclear weapons against Al-Qaeda is that is hard to target them without harming innocent people. The very existence of the terrorist threat and the possibility of nuclear terrorist attacks certainly increase the United Kingdom's government case for replacing the Trident system.

Chapter Three – The End of the Cold War and Beyond

The collapse of the Soviet Union increased concerns that nuclear and other weapons of mass destruction would be supplied to rogue states and terrorist organisations such as Al-Qaeda to use as weapons of terror. It was feared that Russian officials, military personnel and scientists would sell weapons and technology to the highest bidders without regard of the consequences. The guarding of nuclear weapons or radioactive was another cause for concern. On the other hand the demise of the Soviet Union brought the military power of the United States further into the foreground. In theory the United Kingdom would be able to radically reduce if not completely scrap it's nuclear deterrent as the threat to its security was reduced. As discussed above the end of the Cold War did not make the world a more secure place, just a less certain one. Perhaps the best consequence of the Col War had been that it forced the Western Europeans to start integrating with each other improving economic performance and ensuring that they would fight wars amongst themselves again. The down side was that the seemingly unstoppable might of the United States has prompted A-Qaeda to attack American targets. The United Kingdom has supported the war on terror since 9/11 yet the involvement in Iraq could prove to stretch its conventional forces still further as well as using up large segments of the defence budget. Increased instability reduces the incentives for scrapping nuclear deterrents to counter any possible threat.

If taking nuclear deterrence theory to its logical extent then every state would wish to own a nuclear arsenal, presumably leading to a large increase in global proliferation rather than a rationale for disarmament. The main reasons for keeping the United Kingdom's nuclear deterrent are political rather than military. Nuclear weapons are as already mentioned the ultimate political representation of remaining a Great Power as well as giving the ability to wipe out all potential enemies with the exception of the other nuclear powers. Countries such as India and Pakistan have developed nuclear weapons to deter each other yet their weapons are not powerful enough to ensure mutually assured destruction. Therefore they are more likely to use those nuclear weapons against each other,

Pakistan in particular could be tempted as India has much greater conventional forces at its disposal and because India has won the previous war between the two countries. Further proliferation provides excuses for the main nuclear powers to keep their weapons and to update as frequently as needed.

Nuclear weapons have arguably prevented direct military conflicts between the nuclear powers, although conflicts between non-nuclear powers and nuclear powers have still occurred. Non-nuclear powers will gamble that nuclear powers will not use nuclear weapons against them especially if they are closely aligned to another nuclear power. Increases in the destructive power of conventional weapons mean that more conflicts are winnable by conventional arms. Nuclear disarmament would not leave the main nuclear powers defenceless especially if proliferation is stopped completely. At present potential aggressors will gamble on nuclear powers only using conventional weapons against them, as they believe that those nuclear powers are not prepared to face the awful environmental consequences of using nuclear devices. Only the irrational would consider attacking others with nuclear weapons to achieve objectives as those objectives would be destroyed anyway. Whilst it would be valid to constantly update and replace nuclear deterrents to deter those rational enough to be deterred it is irrelevant whether a country has one or thousands of such weapons to those irrational enough not to be deterred by them.

However there are arguments that the United Kingdom does not need a nuclear based key strategic deterrent to replace the Trident system. Those arguments can have a moral, military, economic or political basis. There was always a vocal minority that had always been against the United Kingdom having a nuclear based strategic deterrent and were opposed to each development and continued maintenance of the British nuclear deterrent be it the first atomic bomb of the 1950s or Trident in the 1990s. Most notable amongst the anti-nuclear movement are groups such as the Campaign for Nuclear Disarmament (CND); Friends of the Earth and Greenpeace are against the United Kingdom and all other countries having nuclear weapons. The 1950s had seen the creation of CND, its membership and motivation were revived by the Thatcher government's decision to deploy Trident and allow the Americans to base Cruise missiles at Greenham Common. Developing and maintaining a nuclear replacement for Trident would undoubtedly cause similar demonstrations with a similar inability to stop the government going ahead with such a programme. The Left wing of the Labour Party has traditionally been against the United Kingdom having a nuclear deterrent. The left wing achieved its peak of influence within the Labour Party with the 1983 election manifesto, pledging to decommission Polaris and cancel Trident. The subsequent election defeat convinced the leadership that pledging to scrap Britain's nuclear deterrent is tantamount to electoral suicide and therefore any Labour government would replace Trident with a nuclear system to keep power. The Labour Party leadership however moved away from that unilateral position to retain Trident after regaining office in 1997 and would more than likely adopt a nuclear replacement for Trident as it has pledged to do so in previous election manifestos. Groups such as CND have always felt let down by the Labour Party leadership over its continuation of the United Kingdom nuclear deterrent whenever it has held power.

Other arguments that call for the United Kingdom not to replace Trident with the next generation of submarine based ballistic missiles are based around the ways in which the international, strategic and military situations have changed since the 1990s. Once the Soviet Union collapsed and the Cold War had ended the United Kingdom was not faced with a nuclear power that would specifically target it with nuclear weapons. Whilst the Russian Federation inherited the Soviet Union's nuclear weapons its lack of money forced it to shrink its conventional and nuclear forces. Even though under the presidency of Vladimir Putin the Russians have started to refit and modernise their conventional and nuclear forces they do not pose such a serious threat to British and European security as the Soviet Union did. Given the eastward expansion of both Nato and the European Union the now outwardly capitalist and democratic Russia is further away physically, politically and militarily from posing a threat to Western Europe. Indeed it is in Russia's best interests to build better relationships with the United Kingdom, the European Union and of course the United States.

Although the United Kingdom believes itself to still be a great power its reliance as with the other members of Nato upon the United States in both nuclear and non-nuclear terms is plain to see. Not only did the United States military power sustain Nato during the Cold War it continues to do so. Recent examples include the interventions in Bosnia and Kosovo. The United States dominated the bombing campaign against Serbia in the conflict over Kosovo. The British only contributed some 4% of the planes and munitions used in that conflict.

Those that are opposed to the United Kingdom replacing Trident with a nuclear key strategic deterrent point to the real problems that threaten world peace. For example pressing issues include the environment, pollution, the scarcity and uneven distribution of the world's resources plus the failure to counter health pandemics such as Tuberculosis and AIDS. The reduction of such problems should lessen the risk of terrorism as terrorist groups such as Al-Qaeda use the injustices that the disadvantaged peoples and states face to gain recruits from their midst. If the United Kingdom and other states especially the United States made the world a fairer place then perhaps the world would also become a more peaceful place. In the meantime as the world's finite sources become scarcer then the likelihood of local or regional conflicts over such resources increase. The use or threatened use of nuclear weapons to settle these disputes could lead to the further proliferation of nuclear weapons to states that will not be deterred from using them as they believe they have nothing to lose. The best way that the United Kingdom could stop proliferation is to completely disarm all of its nuclear weapons and urge the other nuclear powers to do the same. As a signatory to the Non Proliferation Treaty of 1968 the United Kingdom alongside the nuclear powers and non-nuclear powers is supposed to be committed to not only preventing nuclear proliferation but also to reducing and eventually scrapping its own nuclear capabilities. It is hypercritical of the nuclear powers to state that they are responsible enough to have nuclear weapons yet those non-nuclear powers are not. Nuclear disarmament groups argue that instead of the United Kingdom and the other nuclear powers replacing their present nuclear systems when they become obsolete that they should scrap them now and spend the money saved on proper decommissioning

programmes and eventually aid projects.
Trident does not have to be replaced in a hurry as long as the Ministry of Defence ensures that refits and equipment upgrades are carried out on a regular basis. From an ethical point of view the morality or immorality of killing thousands or millions of people is not really affected by the means used to kill them. From a military point of view the use of nuclear weapons is more effective in terms of time and resources than using thousands of aircraft to carry the conventional bombs needed to cause the same amount of death and destruction. In any bombing it is difficult to avoid the death of innocent civilians, the best way to avoid such deaths is to prevent conflict in the first place. In political terms nuclear weapons have been acquired to deter others from using theirs. Nuclear weapons are paradoxically only successful if they are not used.

Given that the United Kingdom government will almost inevitably continue to keep the United Kingdom's key strategic deterrent nuclear it will have to keep Trident in service until a replacement has been developed and completed. To achieve this upgrades and refits will be required with as usual the lead for such maintenance and development coming from across the Atlantic. The United States Navy will initially upgrade its Trident D5 missiles and refit its submarines to extend their operational life span before replacing the Trident system completely. The United Kingdom government will have to decide on upgrades and refits prior to deciding to replace Trident just to keep the system viable until the replacement enters service. The Americans are already developing an upgraded version of the Trident D5 as well as contemplating its replacement by the D5EL or the missile currently referred to as the E6. The United Kingdom government may even be able to break its traditional adoption of American missiles to adopt the M51 the missile set to become France's upgraded nuclear deterrent as early as 2010. The adoption of land based ballistic missile and cruise missiles are not currently considered as viable replacements for Trident. Any replacement for Trident may continue the trend to carry fewer warheads that has resulted from lower risks. For instance the United Kingdom has lowered the number of Trident missiles on each submarine from an average of 65 to 58. Its replacement could be less expensive if fewer warheads were needed.

A factor that is not always mentioned with regard to the decommissioning of nuclear weapons is the cost of safely recycling, disposing or storing the radioactive materials. Seen as how the United Kingdom government is more responsible in its attitudes to such a process it can be as expensive to dispose by nuclear systems as it can be to maintain and develop such systems in the first place. For instance the cost of decommissioning the British Army and RAF Lance missiles and WE177 bombs respectively was approximately £23 billion. Given that Trident uses a greater amount of nuclear material the cost could be higher although that could be reduced some of the materials or its replacement's warheads.

Therefore it is very likely that the United Kingdom will decide to develop and maintain a nuclear based key strategic deterrent to replace the Trident system within the 25 years or so. This conclusion is based on the desire of all the United Kingdom governments since 1945to have a nuclear based key strategic deterrent and their determination since 1952 of maintaining the United Kingdom's position as a nuclear power. Originally the United Kingdom could claim that the aim of developing and maintaining a nuclear based key strategic development was to help the United States and Nato remain ahead of the Soviet Union in the nuclear arms race during the Cold War. The United Kingdom government also wished to have nuclear weapons to maintain the country's Great Power status in the face of its seemingly rapid imperial, military and economic decline. The United Kingdom had developed its own nuclear weapons yet since 1958 its main nuclear deterrent systems have come from the United States or been based on American designs. In some respects such reliance on the United States the cost of developing and maintaining of the United Kingdom's nuclear based key strategic deterrent. The decision to replace the Trident system will be mainly based on political criteria rather than upon military ones, although the Royal Navy could be expected to offer advice on the best system to adopt. As for the cost of Trident's replacement it will not be cheap, around £15 billion plus the annual cost of upgrades and refits. Some of these costs could be saved if the Royal Navy decides that it wants a system with lower specifications than the system adopted by the United States Navy. The submarines do not have to have the same number of missile tubes or fewer warheads can be carried.

There are alternatives to adopting another submarine based ballistic missile system to replace Trident although these would not be the first choice of the United Kingdom government, the Ministry of Defence or the Royal Navy. The United Kingdom government could opt for a submarine based nuclear cruise missile system rather than a ballistic missile system. Such a system would have the advantage of being cheaper to develop and maintain as a key strategic deterrent. On the other hand cruise missiles have a shorter range and could only be used against single targets. The United Kingdom government will probably replace the Trident system as much for the potential threats as for actual threats, rather than risk being threatened by states or terrorist organisations. From a strategic point of view it is difficult to predict the future just as the United Kingdom governments of the 1950s could not have predicted the end of the Cold War or the war on terror. A nuclear deterrent will be retained in the hope that other states would be deterred at the prospect of Mutually Assured Destruction. It is a theory based on the assumption that all individuals, organisations and states will always act rationally yet that rationality cannot be guaranteed. It is highly unlikely that the United Kingdom government would abandon its nuclear deterrent in favour of conventional forces as it would not necessarily prove much cheaper than developing and maintaining nuclear weapons, although the costs of safely disposing of nuclear waste would eventually be reduced. Conventional deterrents as history has often shown no not stop conflicts as the consequences of risking war are lower than risking a nuclear confrontation. Of course there will always be people opposed to the United Kingdom replacing the Trident system, yet the Labour and Conservative parties still believe there is more electoral benefits for continuing the nuclear deterrent.

Bibliography

Baldwin T and Evans M 'The hunt for a new nuclear option' The Times May 28 2005.
Bartlett C J (1994) The Global Conflict – The International Rivalry of the Great Powers, 1880-1990 2nd edition, Longman Group UK Limited, Harlow
Benn T (1988) Office without Power –Diaries 1968-72, Arrow Books Limited, London
Bertsch G K and Grillot S R (1998) Arms on the market – reducing the risk of proliferation in the former Soviet Union, Routledge, New York and London
Bonner K & C (2000) Cold War at Sea – an illustrated history, MBI Publishing Company, Osceola
Brown C with Ainley K (2005) Understanding International Relations 3rd edition, Palgrave, Basingstoke
Butler N and Bromley M – Secrecy and dependence: the UK Trident system in the 21st century, Basic Research Report Number 2001.3, November 2001
Carver, Field Marshall Lord (1998) Britain's Army in the 20th Century, Pan strategy guides, London
Castleden R (2005) The World's Most Evil People, Time Warner Books, London and New York
Clarke B (2005) Four Minute Warning – Britain's Cold War, Tempus, Stroud
Comfort N (1993) Brewer's Politics, a phrase and fable dictionary, Cassell, London
DeGroot G (2005) The Bomb – A History of Hell on Earth, Pimlico, London
Evans G & Newnham J (1998) Penguin Dictionary of International Relations, Penguin, London
Goodlad G (2000) British and Imperial Policy 1865-1919, Routledge, London and New York
Greenwood S (2000) Britain and the Cold War 1945-91, Macmillan Press Ltd, Basingstoke
Hill J R (2002) The Oxford Illustrated history of the Royal Navy, Oxford University Press

Hobsbawm, E (1994) Age of Extremes, the Short Twentieth Century 1914-1991, Michael Joseph, London
Hurd D (1997) The Search for Peace - a century of Peace diplomacy, Little Brown & Co, London
Jenkins R (2001) Churchill, Macmillan Press, Basingstoke
Johnston I and McAuley R (2000) The Battleships, 4 Books, London
Kagan R (2003) Paradise & Power
Kennedy P (1976) The Rise and fall of British Naval Mastery, Penguin, London
Kort M (1998) The Columbia Guide to the Cold War, Columbia University Press, New York
Marks S (2003) The Illusion of Peace – International Relations in Europe, 1918-1933 2nd edition, Palgrave Macmillan, Basingstoke
Lennox D – UK options for a strategic nuclear deterrent, 15 September 2005, Jane's.Com
Meir A (2004) Black Earth – Russia after the fall, Harper Perennial, London
Oxford Research Group (15th February 2005) The Future of Britain's Nuclear Weapons: Who decides? Oxford Research Group Consultation, Charney Manor near Oxford, UK December 8-10 2004
Parker R A C (1989) Struggle for Survival – A History of the Second World War
Roberts, J.M (1996)- A History of Europe, Penguin, London
Schama S (2002) A History of Britain Volume 3 – The fate of Empire 1776-2000, BBC Worldwide, London
TruthAndPolitics.org, United States Military Spending – International Comparisons
Van der Vat D (1994) Stealth at Sea – The History of the Submarine, Weidenfeld & Nicholson, London
Watson J (1997) Success in World History since 1945, John Murray, London
Whitmore D C – Abolishing nuclear threats, November 17 1998, Abolishnukes.com
Whitmore D C – Revisiting nuclear deterrent theory, March 1 1998, Abolishnukes.com

Printed in Great Britain
by Amazon